THINKING
OF
SELLING?

The Step By Step Guide To Selling

Your Property

For Top Dollar

HAROLD WOLF

THINKING OF SELLING?

© 2021 **Harold Wolf**

ISBN

First published June 2021
Christine Robinson Global

Disclaimer
This book is presented solely for educational and inspirational purposes.

The author and publisher are not offering it as legal or professional services advice.

While best efforts have been used in preparing this book, the author and publisher make no representations or warranties of any kind and assume no liabilities of any kind with respect to the accuracy or completeness of the contents and specifically disclaim any implied warranties of merchantability or fitness of use for a particular purpose.

Neither the author nor the publisher shall be held liable or responsible to any person or entity with respect to any loss or incidental or consequential damages caused, or alleged to have been caused, directly or indirectly, by the information contained herein.

You should seek the services of a competent professional before acting on any information provided in this book.

Foreword

"I am the basis of all wealth, the heritage of the wise, the thrifty and the prudent.

I am the poor man's joy and comfort, and the rich man's prize, the right hand of capital, the silent partner of many thousands of successful men.

I am the solace of the widow, the comfort of old age, the cornerstone of security against misfortune and want.

I am handed down to children through generations, as a thing of great worth. I am the choicest fruit of toil, credit respects me.

Yet I am humble.

I stand before every man bidding him to know me for what I am and possess me. I grow and increase in value through countless days.

Though I seem dormant, my worth increases, never failing, never ceasing. Time is my aid and population heaps up my gain.

Fire and the elements I defy, for they cannot destroy me.

My possessors learn to believe in me; invariably they become envied. While all things wither and decay, I survive.

The centuries find me younger, increasing in my strength.

I am the foundation of banks, the producer of food and the basis of all wealth throughout the world. Yet I am so common that thousands, unthinking and unknowing, pass me by.

I am Land!"

Unknown Author

Table Of Contents

Introduction

The property market has a pervasive impact not only on Australia's, but the world's economies. It is the popular topic of any number of conversations around gatherings and dinner tables. It generates endless media stories and TV shows.

Property is the cornerstone of governments' revenues and banks' profit margins.

Property is the Great Australian Dream, be it home ownership or investment to create wealth for retirement and to give future generations a head start in life.

Property at large drives the Australian economy and employs a significant proportion of our workforce, whether directly involved in construction and maintenance or supporting industries and their supply chains.

Selling a home is a big decision for most and depending on the circumstances surrounding the sale the seller might see themselves confronted by a myriad of emotions.

Many sellers almost feel overwhelmed when thinking of letting go of their 'castle' and what must be done to achieve a successful outcome.

All the while, they need to take care of their daily lives and routines.

So, when they invite the real estate agent over to start the sales talk, many sellers are mostly troubled by 3 questions:

- What is my home worth?
- What is the sale going to cost me?
- What is the commission rate?

The expected answers to those questions are so dominant on their minds that they often have truly little attention span to what the agent is trying to bring across in their presentation.

All they hope for is to hear a dream price and the lowest marketing and commission rates.

Many sellers choose an agent along these criteria on the assumption that this will deliver them the best financial outcome.

Unfortunately, and usually unknown to the vendor, the loss of that strategy by far outweighs the gain.

So how to avoid the typical mistakes many sellers

make right from the start?

Of course, there are many publications on selling real estate, the internet is loaded with material on the topic.

But it can be confusing and time consuming to find the right information when needed.

To cut through the clutter, the chapters of this book will take you on a step by step journey through the property maze from your initial motivation to sell to handing over the keys to the new owner.

This book is based on my 21 years of experience in the real estate market and is a guide of inspirations and recommendations to lead you to a successful sale.

Sit back and enjoy the read.

1
Getting Started

"The way to get started is to quit talking and begin doing."
Walt Disney

Selling your property is one of the big decisions in your life.

Some people have sold properties in the past, so they might be more familiar with the selling process. Others might sell for the first time or have not sold in a long time. Naturally the question begs: 'Where to Start?'

To get it right, there is quite a long 'To Do' list to follow.

This step by step guide will help you to work through this list in order to make a successful sale.

To promote your property with confidence this book will show you how to price your property in your current market conditions, how to market your property for a successful sale, the costs involved, how to present your property to maximise the sales price, how to research and engage with the best agent, what to understand about the legal process and more.

Before you get started, though, be clear about your intentions and motivation to sell and be open and honest about it with the agent of your choice as this will influence the sales methods and strategies, as well as your decision-making process.

There are a myriad of reasons to sell: debt, death and divorce, upsizing or downsizing, marriage, migration, sea or tree change, you tell me.

Whatever the reasons are, it is most likely an emotional moment to let go of your castle and embrace the next chapter of your life.

Your agent (if you decide to use one) needs to understand the sensitivity of the issue or you need to be sure that you have the emotional strength to manage the sale of your property yourself and jump all sorts of hurdles to achieve the desired result.

Before you read on, though, there is another school of thought: renovating.

This might be a viable alternative, especially if you like where you live and want to stay within the same area because of schools, work, social network or recreation.

Selling and then buying can cost quite some money: preparing your property for sale, marketing, agent and legal fees, stamp duty, more legal fees and makeovers when you buy.

This could already cover a substantial part of the renovation costs; you could turn your house into the home you really want and need while adding a lot of value to your property for now and for future appreciation.

But I guess you got yourself this book because you have decided to move on, so enjoy the read and be inspired.

2

The Best Time To Sell

"Never leave 'till tomorrow that which you can do today."
Benjamin Franklin

One formula applies: sellers are seasonal, buyers are not, no matter where in the property cycle you are selling.

General belief is that the spring selling season from September to December is the best time to sell followed by the autumn selling season from late January until Easter.

You need to consider, though, that the sales price of any product or service is based on the balance of supply and demand.

In the spring and autumn selling seasons more sellers usually compete with each other for the available pool of buyers.

At the very beginning of the year and during the winter months buyers compete over reduced stock levels.

Contrary to the common myth many properties sell better in those so-called off seasons. This is an important consideration especially in the quiet phase of the property cycle.

People often try to time the market to maximise the outcome but mostly miss the moment as all available sales data is always historical.

As a general rule, though, the best time to sell is when you are ready to sell, and the best time to buy is when you are ready to buy.

3

Pricing Your Property For The Market

"Expect the best. Prepare for the worst. Capitalise on what comes."
Zig Ziglar

One of the most essential steps in the sales process is correctly pricing your property.

The old slogan 'location, location, location' only applies to a certain degree.

Other factors, like the state of the economy, planned infrastructure projects or those under construction, population growth, change in demographics, housing supply, vicinity to major road arteries, transport, amenities, education facilities, and easy commute to work all add their own spice to the potential sales price of your property.

What is the neighbourhood like?

Is your address on a busy road or in a quiet leafy street, close to nature, waterways, the beach, or in the middle of suburbia?

The position within its environment is just one part of your home's sales potential, but here, you have little or no control.

Solely in your hands, though, is the condition of the property itself.

Chapters 6 (Preparing your Property for Sale) and Chapter 7 (Open Home Inspections) will cover this topic in more detail, but here are some primary considerations:

- Is the property traditional, heritage or modern?
- Is it well maintained or in need of an update?
- What are its best features?
- Can it be extended?
- What is the backyard like?
- Does it have a pool? Lush and/or well cared landscaping?
- Is there privacy from the neighbours' prying eyes?

Whatever it is, it is up to you to present your property in the best shape possible and make it irresistible for your potential buyer.

Understanding your local market is paramount for both you and your chosen agent.

Also, most buyers nowadays are very well informed as they might have seen many other properties on the market before they stepped into your home.

They have probably done extensive research; all the information on the Internet makes it easy for potential buyers to compare and get an idea of what a property should be worth.

Do your own research before you set your expectations.

Firstly, take the time to inspect other properties advertised for sale in your neighbourhood and see how they compare to your home.

There are now plenty of resources available to help you with price comparisons.

Websites like realestate.com.au, domain.com.au and property reports from the banks are just some of the aids you can use for getting the price right.

The agents you interview are required by law to present you with a 'Comparative Market Analysis' (CMA).

This report compares properties on the number of bedrooms, bathrooms, parking, land size, location, appeal, days on the market and sales prices.

This will help you place your property within the right price range.

Try to be realistic and do not make the pricing of your property an entirely emotional decision.

4
Preparing Your Property For Sale

"Give me six hours to chop down a tree and I will spend the first four sharpening the axe."
Abraham Lincoln

Please have a good hard look at your property and try to see it through your buyers' eyes.

They want to see a well maintained, clean and structurally sound property.

How to present your home as attractive and as inviting as possible depends on its current condition and how much you can afford to give it a makeover, if it looks somewhat tired and does not stack up to other properties on the market.

Here you might face a crucial question: should you renovate or will some tender loving care be sufficient to improve saleability?

A complete renovation is a risky undertaking.

Where should you start? Where should you finish? How much money should you invest?

All too often, the costs blow out because you can count on running into problems that you did not foresee and budget for while you have to live through the mess and inconvenience of a major worksite in progress.

It is hard to recover an overcapitalisation of your property.

You might hope that a renovation notably increases the sales price of your property, but you might in fact turn a significant number of potential buyers away, as they might not like what you have done and will not want to pay for it.

There are plenty of examples where people have gone through the whole renovation blitz, from planning to execution, only to lose money in the end.

Your best may be to leave your home as it is and just spruce up what needs attention and focus on presentation.

Let the new owners sweat the big stuff.

Here are 10 things you can do to prepare your home for photography and open house inspections that won't break the bank, but will add thousands of dollars to the end result:

1. First Impressions Always Count

Even if you cannot afford much, at least give your property a nice kerb appeal.

If people like what they see from the street you have won their first seal of approval.

For example, this could be as simple as cleaning the front façade and front veranda, brushing away dirt and cobwebs, installing a new letterbox and fixing the fence.

Best give the front a new coat of paint, repair anything that needs attention like facias and shutters, gutters and downpipes, tiles or deck timbers, manicure the front garden and add a few colourful plants.

Want to invite buyers in? Bring your kerbside appeal to life!

https://theinteriorsaddict.com/

2. Declutter - Less Is More

Potential buyers do not come to admire your possessions.

Clean, uncluttered spaces act as a blank canvas and help potential buyers imagine how their own furnishings might fit and look.

Let's be honest; everyone's home is filled with 'stuff', from things we haven't bothered putting away to things we cherish like memorabilia, family and holiday photos, the magnetic sticker collection on the fridge, collectables, trophies, children's toys, pieces of furniture ... the list goes on.

All this must disappear, apart from a few chosen

pieces that help with presentation.

Go through your whole house with a fine toothcomb and start packing, clearing out cupboards and organising your closets; it will make your home look more spacious.

Most importantly, put valuables out of sight.

People will open wardrobe doors and drawers and you won't have time to look over everyone's shoulders.

Rent a storage unit to store away all your boxes and everything that is not necessarily needed while you are in the selling phase.

It might pay off to engage a stylist, as they can make your place look sensational just with some of the things you already have.

To the other extreme, they might recommend you completely empty your house and display furnish it to match the character of your home and the era it was built.

Just some food for thought.

Before

After

3. The Paint Job

Now with all that 'stuff' and possibly some furniture gone, any wear and tear will be more obvious. A new coat of paint is the easiest, fastest and cheapest way to freshen up your home.

While painting, scratches and cracks can be filled in and old picture hooks can be removed.

There is no need for any fancy feature walls; a neutral warm off-white tone will do and will go well with any style of decoration.

It will also make the house look brighter.

If you are not handy enough or pressed for time, call in the professionals.

They have all the right gear and the whole job can be finished in 2 or 3 days, depending on how much needs to be done.

Image: https://simplemadepretty.com

What a difference painting the walls, changing the floorcovering and styling with furniture makes ... not to mention the $$$ value added.

4. Scrub Every Nook and Cranny

If your back allows, scrub down every inch of your property. Otherwise, call in a cleaner.

Remove every bit of dirt, stain, mould, treat timbers and polish metals, remove the dirt from the rolling tracks of slider doors and spray in a little WD40 so that the doors slide back and forth with ease.

Ensure that all your appliances like the oven, microwave and dishwasher, taps, door handles, sinks and toilets shine and sparkle.

Clean all windows, mirrors and shower screens, picture rails and any surfaces.

No matter the state of repair of your property, it needs to be spotless inside and outside.

5. Everyone Loves the Great Outdoors

Many house hunters walk straight through your property and first have a look at the backyard. They are thinking of recreation, entertaining and room for the kids and pets to roam around. Clean, prune, weed, mulch or add some pot plants if you only have a courtyard.

Cut back plants in front of windows to let more light into the house.

Get rid of the old rusty clothesline and remove any debris that is lying around. Make sure the fence is in good repair, and the back gate locks.

Oil the timber deck if dry and weather-worn.

Again, simplicity is the key to make your outdoor space inviting.

Image: https://www.boredpanda.com/

Quickly transform even a small corner of your garden with paint and furniture that you can take with you, or you can hire.

6. Make Sure Everything Works Fine

Check everything that moves, rolls, slides, turns, flicks, flips, switches, swivels, opens, closes, locks, unlocks, heats, cools, illuminates or darkens.

Nothing is worse than loose door handles, leaking taps and blinds hanging at half-mast. People see this as a sign of neglect and poor maintenance.

Make sure all doors and windows close properly and can be locked and that all taps turn easily and get a plumber to renew any leaky washers.

People test these things; they flush the toilets, open and close slider and wardrobe doors and switch lights on and off.

So be sure that all power points, lights and light switches work, and there are no wires sticking out anywhere.

Replacing the faceplates of light switches and power points is a small attention to detail with a big impact.

Replace all blown light bulbs and downlights and test the fire alarms. Check the garage remote and make sure the air conditioner does not leak. Ensure that all the kitchen appliances and curtains or blinds work.

Again, it's best to get a plumber, an electrician or a handyperson to check your property from top to bottom and attend to everything that needs fixing.

Whatever your budget might be, presentation tips 1 to 6 are an absolute must if you want to compete with other properties on the market and if you want to attract buyers' recognition.

It also will be very tough to achieve a satisfying sales result unless you are lucky enough to sell in a booming market where buyers snap up anything they can get their hands on.

But these times are rare.

So better roll up your sleeves and apply some elbow grease.

If you have some extra money to splash around here are some more tips on how you can add value to your home without the need for jackhammers.

7. Kitchens Sell Houses

The kitchen is the most important room in the house.

Most house hunters will have a close look at the kitchen, especially women, checking the cupboards, trying the drawers and scrutinising the appliances.

A great deal of family life happens in the kitchen so if you think of any renovation, this is the place to start.

You do not necessarily have to replace the whole kitchen, but you should be closely examine a few items for renewal:

- Benchtop
- Taps
- Cupboard door handles
- Splashback
- Cooktop
- Oven
- Rangehood
- Microwave
- Dishwasher

It is your judgment call, but it is best to consult an agent or a stylist to what extent you should go with any renovation ideas.

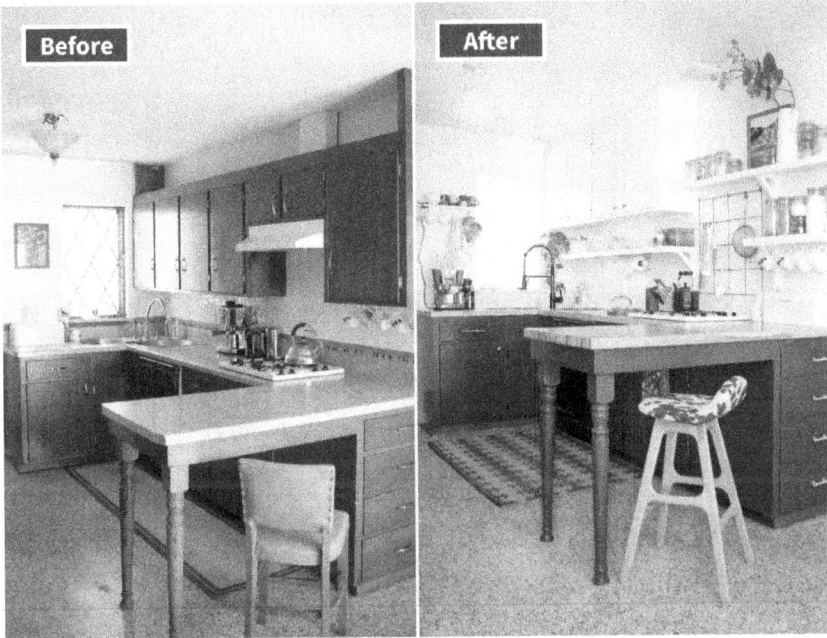

Bring your kitchen into the 21st century with some paint and shelving

Images: https://www.boredpanda.com/

8. The Bathroom – Do Not Disturb

A bathroom is a place of private time and serenity.

Renewing a whole bathroom is an expensive exercise, but replacing the 'throne' is fairly easy to do. Tile paint and a new bathtub coating will give your bathroom a clean and fresh look.

If you have a shower curtain, get a new one.

Maybe new taps and a new mirror, but the rest is pretty much just about decoration.

9. New Floorcoverings – Please Take Your Shoes Off

No matter what you might be doing to spruce up your home, a worn-out carpet full of stains or a tired, scratched up timber floor will reduce all your efforts to present your home nicely.

If the carpet is new or the floorboards are freshly polished, you can ask your potential buyers to take their shoes off before entering; this will earn your house a great first impression and a great deal of respect.

10. Window Dressings – The Right for Privacy

Blinds or curtains make a home look cosy, and without them, a house looks naked.

They not only keep out summer heat or winter cold, but also prying eyes from neighbours and passers-by.

Window dressings give the residents privacy and

protection, and your potential buyers will appreciate this attention to detail.

Do not forget the flyscreens. If you have them make sure they are clean and in good order.

If you have roller shutters, make sure they work.

I hope you get the picture.

I am trying to inspire you to look at your property with an open mind and a critical eye.

Decide for yourself how much you want, or how far you can extend yourself to bring your property to showroom condition.

In this respect, consider what had attracted you or turned you off when you researched the market and looked at other properties for sale.

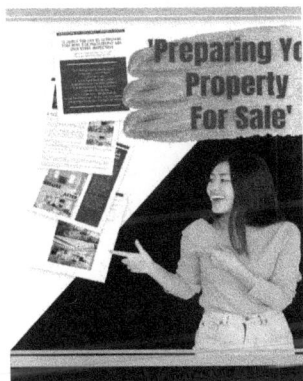

I have prepared a PDF of *Preparing Your Property For Sale* with some further info you can download from this link

www.realestate4u.com.au/ bonus

5

Successful Marketing

"Think like a wise man but communicate in the language of the people."
William Butler Yeats

The three most pressing questions every home seller has on their mind are:

- What is my property worth?
- What is the sales commission?
- How much are the marketing costs?

Chapter 11 (The Costs of a Successful Sale) will cover these details, but the age-old rule applies:

You Get What You Pay For!

The primary aim of marketing is to attract as many

buyers as possible.

Like a fisherman needs to cast a big net if he wants to catch many fish, so the marketing of your property needs to reach out as far as possible to create sufficient competition.

Saving on marketing investment is nothing more than trying to sell a secret.

If potential buyers do not know that you are selling, you will not get the competition you need to maximise your sales result.

Successful marketing is based on Reach and Frequency.

'**Reach**' means how many people will see your property advertised.

'**Frequency**' means how many times they will see it promoted.

First things first, though, you need to prepare your property for presentation, which will be discussed in more detail in the next chapter.

Professional Photography

Quintessential in attracting potential buyers are professional photography, a floor plan with measurements and a professionally written copy text.

In the face of competition, video and virtual tours of a property become more and more the norm as essential pre-inspection tools.

Remember, you are selling an important financial asset, and it is all about first impressions.

A few DIY shots on your smartphone will not cut it; professional photography and filming is a must.

On photography day, your property needs to present in showroom condition; the garden perfectly manicured, not the slightest mess anywhere and remember, Less Is More.

Also, make sure you pick a bright, sunny day, choosing the time when your property shines in the best natural light.

Reschedule the photo appointment if the day turns out grey and rainy.

Reach

The internet has become the most essential marketing tool.

In the online world, two major websites compete for your business: realestate.com.au and domain.com.au (in Australia).

Each of these sites has its following.

If you want to give your property the widest possible exposure, you need to advertise on both. There is no way around it.

A new player in the world of advertising is Social Media.

Facebook, Instagram, Twitter and LinkedIn are taking the world by storm, and you have got to be in it to win it.

Some people might tell you that social media marketing comes for free, but this is not the case if you want to reach out to a large and targeted audience.

But the costs are within reasonable limits, compared to the potential impact. Some people might also tell you that social media marketing does not work.

Done correctly, it might be the most (cost) effective advertising media there is.

Nearly all buyers these days start their house hunting online.

Modern devices like smartphones, tablets and laptop computers allow people to search on the go and shortlist those properties they really like to see in the flesh.

People are also pressed for time and rarely scroll past the first one or two website pages, so your property needs to show up right on the top of the search pages and stand out from the pack, with stunning photos and focus on the features and benefits.

The times of expensive printed media advertising are pretty much over, as only a few people nowadays flick through the local newspapers or glossy weekly magazines to find their next home or investment.

Frequency

Experts say that we need to be exposed to a product or service up to 8 times or more before we memorise it.

Here is how you get into your potential buyers' heads that many times:

- Online Advertising
- Automatic E-Brochure upon an Internet Enquiry
- The Follow Up Call or Email Response, if contact details are provided
- Social Media Marketing
- Printed Media (in selected areas and if the

expense makes sense)
- Agent DataBase Marketing
- Video Presentation and Virtual Tours in addition to Photography
- Letterbox Drops
- The Signboard
- Agency Window Displays
- Viewing the property at Open House Inspections
- The Brochure, handed out at Open Inspections
- The Energy, Enthusiasm and Objection-Handling Skills of the person presenting the property to potential buyers
- The Follow Up Calls after the inspection appointments
- The Contract of Sale
- The Strata Report for units or Building and Pest Inspection Report for houses

Now let me explain this list in plain English:

Ask yourself, when you bought the property that you are now selling (and you might already be searching for your next one), where did you,and do you still, see property advertised?

Maybe you bought the existing home before the times of online advertising. But for your next purchase, you are most likely surfing the net.

And so are all house hunters these days.

An E-Brochure can be automatically sent out to both realestate.com.au and domain.com.au databases of registered corresponding buyers, depending on your available marketing budget.

Most agents withhold some information from web advertisements to entice potential buyers to contact them, providing the agent with their contact details.

This is the first important skill in the sales process; an opportunity to engage with potential buyers in email or telephone conversations, extract vital information and urge them to attend the next Open House Inspection without spilling all the beans.

The same goes for marketing your property on Social Media, Printed Media, and an agent's database, if you choose to employ an agent (discussed later in Chapter 9, Choosing the Right Agent).

Video Presentations and Virtual Tours of your home will set you apart from your competitors in the market and enhance curiosity amongst potential buyers.

Letterbox Drops might be old school marketing but can attract potential buyers; especially from the closer neighbourhood who are not necessarily active house hunters, but decide to take advantage of an unexpected opportunity, or recommend your property to someone they would like to have close by, like parents, kids, a relative or good friends.

The Signboard, also called the '24-hour Salesman', lets your neighbours and passers-by know that you are selling and helps potential buyers to locate your property in the street easily.

The Open House Inspection: this is the most crucial moment in your marketing campaign and your opportunity to make potential buyers fall in love with your home (which we will talk more about in Chapter 7, Open Home Inspections).

The Follow-Up Call after the inspection is the most important sales call (discussed further in Chapter 8, DIY or Agent).

The requests for a Contract of Sale and strata or building and pest inspection reports are the legal components in a buyer's decision-making process and can make or break a deal (covered in Chapter 13, The Legal Process).

That is how you draw a crowd; the more people that turn up at open house inspections, the more competition you will create.

The more people that like your property, the bigger the chance of achieving an outstanding sales result.

And this is what the marketing of your property is all about: Creating Competition.

6
Selling Methods

"How you sell is more important than what you sell."
Andy Paul

There are 5 commonly used methods of selling a property:

1. Expression of Interest (EOI)
2. Off Market
3. Private Treaty
4. Public Auction
5. 'Market Buy' or 'Openn Negotiations'

EOI is a method of selling high-end properties for reasons of privacy and anonymity, and other special conditions.

Sellers only want serious and qualified buyers coming through their property, and potential buyers usually want to stay anonymous.

Buyers are invited to make their best and final offer and any buying conditions in writing, in an enclosed envelope, before a specific date.

On the expiry of the deadline, the envelopes are opened and the seller decides who they want to sell their property to. This might not be the buyer submitting the highest price but could be someone offering certain buying conditions that are in the seller's interest.

If neither the price offer nor the purchase condition meet the seller's expectations, the property can be put back onto the market using any of the 5 selling methods.

Off Market sales are made without a public marketing campaign to buyers on an agent's database of buyers, or where the seller cannot or does not want to afford the costs of an advertising campaign.

Unless the agent has one or several serious buyers, the downside of this method is the lack of competition.

It is hard to 'sell a secret' and this method is not suitable for a DIY seller.

Private Treaty is the most common method of sale. It is also the preferred sales method of most buyers as usually a price or price guide is given, and an interested buyer can directly negotiate the sales price with the seller, potentially avoiding competition with other buyers. It also relieves buyers from the emotional roller coaster of an auction sale.

More so, a private treaty sale provides the opportunity to exchange contracts for sale with a cooling-off period (except Tasmania) and a small termination fee (except NT) in case the buyer decides to back out of the contract (see Chapter 16, Real Estate Terminology, for what applies in your state).

In NSW, for example, a holding deposit of 0.25% of the purchase price is payable at exchange of contracts and will be forfeited to the vendor if the purchaser decides to rescind the Contract of Sale.

Reasons for rescission of contract could be a strata or building report revealing problems with the property, the bank disapproving the finance application, the bank valuation not confirming the purchase price or simply a change of heart by the buyer. The seller, however, is bound by the contract and cannot sell the property to another purchaser who might offer a better price while the contract is in the cooling period.

This means that the seller could potentially lose both buyers and experience a disruption to their marketing campaign. In other words, in a Private Treaty sale, the buyer has the upper hand and controls the process.

In a **Public Auction**, your property is offered for sale through a competitive bidding process. It is a great sales method in the high demand markets of our capital cities and busy rural centres. It is also the most transparent sales method and the best way to determine the true market value of a property.

The main advantages of an auction sale are:

- The auction date, usually 4-5 weeks, sets a time limit, and interested purchasers must do their due diligence, review the contract for sale and arrange their finance before the auction date.
- Interested buyers openly compete with each other in a transparent bidding process.
- The emotional charge of an auction often drives up the final sales price.
- The reserve price ensures that the property is not undersold and is confidential only to the seller, the agent (if any) and the auctioneer.
- Once the reserve price is reached or exceeded the winning bid is binding for both buyer and seller, and the purchaser (or their represen- tative) has to sign the Contract of Sale and

hand over a 10% deposit on the spot.

- There is no cooling-off period, and the Contract of Sale is unconditional and legally binding for both buyer and seller.

Pre-auction offers can be accepted if they are attractive enough, and contracts are exchanged under auction conditions with a cooling-off waiver (66W certificate signed by the buyer's legal representative).

If the auction fails to achieve a result, the process converts into a Private Treaty sale and usually the sale is made within the following few days to one of the interested or registered parties of the auction.

In a public auction, the seller controls the process.

Another sales method – **'Market Buy'** or **'Openn Negotiations'**– is lately gaining tremendous popularity. It is a hybrid version of a sale by Private Treaty and Auction, similar to eBay. There is a transparent bidding process, but without an auctioneer.

Interested buyers have more time to place their bids and can also add certain purchase conditions, like early or delayed settlement or exchange of contracts with a cooling-off period, to name a few examples. Buyers can see the bids of other buyers, if any, which eliminates the suspicion of being strung along by the sales tactics of an agent who might be 'economical with the truth'.

The main advantages of this sales method are:

- Placed offers, including purchase conditions, are transparent for every potential buyer to see.
- Only genuinely interested buyers are invited by the agent to participate in the process.
- The seller can nominate a reserve price that remains confidential.
- Once an offer has been accepted by the seller, contracts need to be exchanged within 24 hours under the agreed purchase conditions.

7

Setting The Reserve Price

"You know you're priced right when your customers complain – but buy anyway."
John Harrison

The reserve price is the lowest price you are willing to accept on auction day.

Your agent has hopefully provided you with the feedback from all the open inspection attendees, or you have asked the questions yourself if you are a DIY seller.

Here are some of the important questions to ask potential buyers:

- Are you interested in buying this property?

- Have you forwarded the Contract of Sale to your lawyer or conveyancer for review?
- Have you completed your due diligence?
- Is your finance approved and a 10% deposit ready?
- Do you want to forward a pre-auction offer?
- Are you familiar with the auction process?
- Are you aware that in an auction there is no cooling-off period?

A good indication of potential competition on auction day is the amount of second inspections and building inspections during the marketing campaign, the number of contracts issued and more so, how many potential buyers have requested adjustments to the Contract for Sale through their legal representative. The latter means they have already engaged a solicitor or conveyancer to review the contract and paid money for that service. They are your most serious contenders and most likely to register for the auction.

Set the reserve price somewhat higher than the buyer feedback, as you can always lower it during the auction to meet the market if necessary, but you cannot increase it once the auction is under way.

As a general rule, balance the market feedback with your own financial needs to move on with life after the sale and make a calculated and informed decision about your desired outcome.

Set the reserve by staying business minded and leaving emotions aside.

8

Open For Inspection (OFI)

"Buyers decide in the first eight seconds of seeing a home if they're interested in buying it. Get out of your car, walk in their shoes and see what they see within the first eight seconds."
Barbara Corcoran

IT'S SHOWTIME!

All the work done (or not done) from the previous chapters will now come together and you will inevitably face the scrutiny of potential buyers.

Before opening the front door for inspection walk through your property from front to back one last time and see it through your buyers' eyes. Perhaps ask a friend to do the same.

Give it a last sweep and de-clutter, removing any things lying around from shoes to clothes to kids' toys, mail in the hallway, pets' paraphernalia, etc.

Tidy up drawers and closets and most of all hide away any valuables like jewellery, phones, tablets, laptop computers and small precious items that can easily disappear in a pocket or handbag.

Temptation can make thieves.

Some stylists offer to come to your property before the inspection and give it a last dress up and makeover. This might be a small expense very well invested.

Switch on the lights, open the curtains and blinds, flip down the toilet lids, turn the heater on in winter and the air conditioner in summer for a comfortable temperature (not too hot or not too cold), light lightly scented candles and turn on some calming and soothing music.

If you really want to impress your potential buyers, have some light snacks prepared on the kitchen bench top together with some fresh lemonade. And the smell of freshly baked home-made biscuits provide a real homely and comforting aroma.

It is a great way to hold people for a bit longer before they move on to the next property and get some vital information from them.

Schedule your OFI times:

Saturdays mid-morning to mid-afternoon are popular times for OFI. Check the opening times of other properties in your neighbourhood and set your viewing schedule apart from theirs, otherwise buyers will just rush through as not to miss the inspection times of your competitors.

If you really want to maximise it, open up on Sundays late morning, as well.

Some house hunters work on Saturdays or have religious constraints, but on Sundays they have time and do not have to rush.

Late afternoons in the middle of the week work well, so people can stop by after work or can see what your property looks like in twilight. This works particularly well if you have nice views.

And, of course, be flexible to allow for inspections by appointment. Some people like to avoid the typical inspection trail and take their time, especially when they come for a second inspection.

A second inspection means that this person has your property on their shortlist, which is one of the critical moments in your marketing campaign, as a potential offer or pre-auction offer might not be far away.

First impressions always count but bring out the absolute best of your property for a second inspection, as this house hunter will now have a more thorough look to make sure they did not miss anything the first time around.

If you are using an agent, leave the property well before inspection time allowing the agent to have a last check and set themselves up and fly the 'Open for Inspection' flag.

House hunters usually do not like the owners being present; they might feel that they cannot speak openly about aspects they dislike without intimidating the owner. The nervous tension of an owner watching potential buyers is not helping the agent either; it's counterproductive.

This might be your predicament if you decide to go DIY.

I attend DIY inspection appointments and find the owners almost freeze when asking for personal details. Or they oversell with endless talk to avoid critical questions, as they are inexperienced in handling objections.

This is the biggest hurdle for DIY sellers as they often take the critique of house hunters at open inspections personally and do not know how to deal with the feedback, while an experienced agent is emotionally detached from the property and knows how to handle these situations to your advantage.

Which leads us to the next chapter: Using an Agent or Do It Yourself?

9

Using An Agent Or Do It Yourself

"Challenges are what make life interesting and overcoming them is what makes life meaningful."
Joshua J. Marine

So far, you could argue that you could complete all of the above yourself by ticking off a checklist if you have the time, knowledge and resources.

What could be your reason, though, for going it alone: saving the sales commission, or proving to yourself that you can do a better job than an agent?

The opinion that agents just try to look good at OFIs, write down names and telephone numbers, and that property basically sells itself is a huge myth and massive misconception.

What sellers don't see is the work an agent does behind the scenes, project managing everything and everyone needed to ensure a successful sale, getting your marketing materials distributed, liaising with legal and finance professionals and most of all, talking to all potential buyers, from online and phone enquiries to data-base clients and those who attended the open house inspections.

This means many hours of (often repeated) phone calls, asking questions, engaging the person on the other end of the line in a conversation to find out their likes and dislikes of your property and handling their objections, enticing them to come for a second inspection, talking about their finances and ultimately trying to get an offer out of them.

Organising an auction is another task where no stone can be left unturned. Every potential buyer needs to be reminded to do their research, have the Contract of Sale reviewed by their legal representative, have their finance ready and the deposit cheque with them.

Auctioneers often visit the property before the auction, see it for themselves and chat with the vendor to ensure that they are familiar with the process and understand the vendor bid and the reserve price.

During the auction the agent's most difficult job is communicating with every buyer who is participating in the bidding process and making them increase their bids.

This skill has been learned, practised and refined countless times in training sessions and on the job experience and is impossible to be applied by an owner seller.

Even many agents struggle with it.

This is all part of the negotiation and competition creating process.

You need to honestly ask yourself: "Do I have the time, skills and expertise to live up to this challenge?"

Are you confident enough to take the place of an experienced agent while you are most likely engaged enough with your own life?

Selling real estate is no part-time job, otherwise, everyone could (and would) do it. And there are legal and statutory requirements to comply with in every property transaction.

Last but not least, as a DIY seller, you can only advertise on domain.com.au and some minor web portals, thus missing out on about half of all potential purchasers.

This is what you risk by choosing against agent support.

10

Choosing The Right Agent

"Success in business requires training and discipline and hard work. But if you're not frightened by these things, the opportunities are just as great today as they ever were."
David Rockefeller

This is the most difficult chapter to write about; now, it is about your emotions and perceptions, your communication skills and your intuition.

This chapter is about you trusting your gut instinct and making the right decision in choosing the right agent.

Real estate agents come from all walks of life and in all shapes, forms, sizes and characters.

Some have started in the industry after finishing high school, some have university degrees, some have crossed over from other professions and some grew up with their parents already running an agency.

There are young go-getters and mature aged professionals.

There are agents new to the industry and those with years of experience.

There are agents that smile from many sales and advertisement boards and there are the quiet achievers.

There is the more serious, quiet type and the fast talker.

But when you narrow it down, there are only two types of agents: those who care for your best interest and those who foremost think of their own bank balance.

So, how do you pick the one that is right for you?

Always interview at least three agents.

Have a list of questions ready to ask each one of them and compare their answers. Make notes of their responses and how they make you feel.

Do not be shy; these are important interviews, so make them earn your business.

The agents that have your best interest at heart will ask a lot of detailed questions. They want to know what motivates you to sell, they want to know your concerns and what you expect from them, they want to know what you love about your property, they take their time to get to know you and your property, understand you and earn your trust.

They provide you with detailed, current information about the state of the market in your suburb and even in your street so that you get the pricing right.

They outline, in detail, the selling methods and marketing and options available, make their recommendations and help you make an informed decision about how to proceed. They make you feel at ease and respected, as they understand that putting your property up for sale is a big decision for you.

On the other hand, the other lot beat their own chests with their grand achievements and successes. They talk about themselves and tell you everything you like to hear. They usually talk and give you little airtime; no other agent will do a better job than them, and their price estimate is almost too good to be true (and usually is).

When they stand or sit across from you beaming with confidence and energy, you will know what I mean. You will feel the pressure they are putting you under as they are determined to leave the appointment with a signed agency agreement in their pocket.

Here are 10 questions I suggest you use as a guideline:

1. How long have you been a real estate agent?

Keep an open mind. There is the experienced negotiator with years of industry experience who might have become a bit complacent versus the newcomer, enthusiastic and working hard to achieve a great outcome and build their reputation.

2. Have you sold any similar properties recently?

They might already have some suitable buyers for your property on their database and your property could potentially be sold off market and save you time and the advertising expenses.

Of course, only if the price is right.

3. Is there currently demand for my kind of property?

This of course depends on the kind of property you are selling, and the possible outcome will depend on the current supply of similar properties nearby.

4. Are you a local agency?

Principally any agent can sell your property. But how well does the 'out of towner' know your market?

How many comparable properties have they seen so they can distinguish and talk comparison with potential buyers?

How many potential buyers do they have on their database looking in your suburb?

5. How do you differ from your competitors?

Frustrated sellers often comment that they rarely hear from their agent. Find out how often they will communicate with you and in which way. Will they send you regular written reports or just fill you in on the phone? What information will they provide you?

Are they working alone or in a team?

What does it mean to them 'to go the extra mile'?

Most importantly, ask for written testimonials to see what previous clients have to say.

RateMyAgent.com.au is a useful source of testimonials as they are written by the actual buyers and sellers; the agent cannot edit them to their liking. For example, you can see my testimonials by clicking on *Agents* and typing my name *Harold Wolf, Sydney*.

6. What marketing plan are you recommending, and how much will it cost?

The costs for comparable marketing plans should be essentially identical.

The two major web portals charge similar prices to all agencies in the same area.

There could be a slight cost variation for photography and print material depending on which suppliers are used.

If a similar marketing plan costs lots more than the others, ask why.

7. Which sales method would you recommend and why?

An experienced agent will explain the differences to you.

An agent who prefers auctions is usually a good negotiator in Private Treaty Sales but not necessarily the other way round.

Running a successful auction campaign needs practice, experience and confidence with the process. However, it also depends on the address of your property. In certain areas auction sales are the norm; they do not work in other areas, as potential buyers are uncertain of the process.

It also depends on the type of property.

If you are selling a small studio or 1 bedroom apartment and your target market is First Home Buyers, these buyers might not be able to bid at auction because of banking restrictions.

'Market Buy' is a suitable alternative to Private Treaty sales, as explained earlier in the book. Find out whether the agent has a subscription to the model and is familiar with it.

8. What do you think the property will sell for?

Here you can separate the wheat from the chaff because who can really predict the outcome?

If you have done enough research yourself and stay objective, you should already have a fair idea of what your home should be worth.

The agent needs to substantiate their price assessment with a Comparative Market Analysis, which is a list of similar properties that have sold in the recent past in your neighbourhood, and not just pick a figure out of thin air.

The honest agent will give you a price range, a mix of historical data and their knowledge of the current market and buyer sentiment.

The self-centred agent will tell you what they think you want to hear, which is the number that seems too good to be true.

The real sales result, however, will depend on the motivation of the buyers that are house hunting at the time when your property comes onto the market, the frequency and reach of your marketing campaign, the sales method, the competition between interested buyers and how well your agent manages the whole process.

9. What would be your catchphrase when selling my home?

The agent might not necessarily be a good copywriter.

But if they have asked you enough questions about the features and benefits of your property and have listened well enough to your answers and taken notes, they should be able to sell your property back to you in a few short sentences.

If it works for you it will work on prospective buyers, and this will then be the basis for a professional copywriter to come up with a compelling advertisement script.

10. *What commission rate do you charge?*

That is one of the most pressing questions on any seller's mind, and the old saying prevails:

You get what you pay for!

Many sellers make the crucial mistake to choose an agent on a commission rate and usually opt for the cheapest one.

Would you pick the cheapest doctor, dentist, accountant, car mechanic ...?

Most likely not, as you would naturally doubt whether you will get the best service.

Knowing what they are worth, an experienced and confident agent will quote you at the upper end of the rate scale in your area.

They might be willing to negotiate a little bit, but the thing is, if they buckle under your pressure, they will most likely give in to the negotiation skills of the buyer as well.

And this is not in your best interest.

The cheap agent is likely to be desperate to win business, and their head might be occupied more with their personal circumstances rather than with creating the best result for you.

If you are willing to pay someone well, they will be loyal, work hard and go the extra mile to achieve the best possible outcome for you. They will feel they owe you one. And this is what you want, as this will determine how you can move forward into the future.

Of course, the commission rates are not the same everywhere. Each state has its own rules and regulations, so you need to check what applies in your neck of the woods.

A good idea is to negotiate a tiered commission rate: a certain percentage up to the most likely sales price of the property and a bonus rate for anything above.

Example:

For argument's sake, all research indicates that your property should sell for $1M, and you would be happy with that result.

The agent quotes you a commission rate of 2%, hence the selling fee at a sales result of $1M would amount to $20,000.

Offer the agent a 1.8% commission up to $1M and 10%

in every dollar from thereon.

If the property sells at the expected $1M their fee would be $18,000, so you saved yourself $2000.

However, if the property sells at $1,050,000, the agent earns an extra 10% on those $50,000, which is $5000, so the sales commission adds up to $23,000 ($18,000 + $5000) for the agent.

And you make an extra $45,000.

Everyone wins, and the agent sees an incentive to work and negotiate just a bit harder.

11

Working With Your Agent

"Tell me and I forget. Teach me and I remember.
Involve me and I learn."
Benjamin Franklin

You have decided to team up with an agent, now it's time to work as a team. Like in all healthy relationships, communication is the key to success.

Of course, the onus is on the agent to keep you properly informed along the way.

You may have questions or concerns, so better voice them immediately instead of dwelling on them and letting them grow into sores.

Do your best to support the agent and prepare the property into 'showroom' condition before every open inspection.

Listen to your agent's suggestions; they know what works with buyers and what does not. You might disagree but it is nothing personal; the less the house hunter can critique, the more likely you are to get a great sales result within a reasonable timeframe.

All sellers hope to get the sale done ASAP, as selling a home is an emotional moment in life.

But not all properties sell within the first few weeks of campaigning, especially in Private Treaty sales.

This can be for a number of reasons, for instance:

- The right buyer has not turned up yet, or they don't like the sales process.
- Some similar properties have come up for sale in the vicinity and steal interest from your property.
- It might be a pricing issue.
- There might be unexpected economic changes.
- You simply can't afford the TLC your property would need.

Whatever it is, do not lose patience, keep talking to your agent, be open to make some adjustments, ignore the phone calls you might get from other agents and stay focused, your day will come.

Worst case scenario may be that your property is on the market for too long and it is better to give it a break for a while and come back at another time.

This could also mean choosing another agent; fresh blood with fresh energy and new buyers in the market might bring you the desired result the second time around.

12

The Costs Of A Successful Sale

"If you are not willing to risk the usual, you will have to settle for the ordinary."
Jim Rohn

Successfully selling your property comes with some costs. But rather than seeing them as an expenditure, see them as an investment into yourself to achieve the desired outcome.

Here are the items you will have to spend money on:

Preparing the Property for Sale (Chapter 6)

This of course depends on your budget and the extent of work your property needs to present well. This can be between zero and five or six figures, depending on what you can do yourself and where you need professional help.

Talk to your agent and establish a to-do list using Chapter 6 (Preparing Your Property for Sale) as a guideline.

Sometimes, it really is just rolling up your sleeves and applying some elbow grease.

Legal Representation

You need to engage a solicitor or conveyancer to draw up a Contract of Sale. In some states such as SA, the agent can do this with zero additional fees.

Depending on the complexity of the contract their fees might be between $1000 and $5000. Get a few quotes and compare. If you do not know anyone your agent can surely refer you.

Marketing Budget (Chapter 5)

Every dollar spent here will contribute to the success and result of your sale.

Your agent should have a couple of options available but fundamentally these are the important pieces of the puzzle:

Photography and floor plan	$300 - $500
Video & Virtual Tour	$300 - $500
Professional Copy Writer	$200 - $500
Sign Board (simple – solar board)	$350 - $750
Colour Brochures	$300 - $800
Real Estate.com.au	$1,700-$2,300 (Highlight Property)
Domain.com.au	$1,900 - $2,700 (Premium Plus)
Social Media	$500 - $1000
Auctioneer	$550 - $1200
Admin & InHouse Printing	$300 - $500

(The quotes above are an approximate guideline only.)

DIY sellers will have to source all service providers themselves and might pay more for some of them than for the agent referred professionals.

As already mentioned, DIY sellers cannot advertise on realestate.com.au as only subscribed agents can use this platform. This means that DIY sellers are losing out on about 50% of market reach.

Your agent will provide you with an exact break up of their marketing options and it will depend on the type of property you are selling and your target market when deciding which option makes the best sense.

Just remember, advertisement is about presentation, reach and frequency (as outlined in Chapter 5). The less you are willing to spend, the fewer people you will reach and attract. This will have an impact on the competition between buyers you want to create and therefore determine the end result.

In this instance, less is definitely **Not** more.

Do not entertain the thought of making the agent pay for your marketing expenses. You might think that this inspires the agent to work harder, but all you are doing is creating a conflict of interest for them.

Just imagine an agent owes money for a number of marketing campaigns on their credit card. Their head will be in money recovery mode and they will inevitably try to close those deals as quickly as possible.

Every day the properties are not sold will cost them interest, hence fighting for the best possible price is not at the top of their agenda.

13

The Art Of Negotiations

"Believe you can and you're halfway there."
Theodore Roosevelt

'SHOW ME THE MONEY'

Let us set off with the refrain from the famous Kenny Rogers song 'The Gambler':

"You've got to know when to hold 'em
Know when to fold 'em
Know when to walk away
And know when to run
You never count your money
When you're sittin' at the table
There'll be time enough for countin'
When the dealin's done"

Like in poker, negotiating the best price for your property is about skills and who has the strongest nerves.

The agent stands in between the seller and the purchaser, and their job is to bring the two parties together in an agreement.

Successful negotiating is not only an art that takes time to develop, it is also a talent that some people have and some do not.

Negotiating is an emotional roller coaster, from the fear of missing out and letting go to plain greed. It might not be easy to keep your emotions in check. Most importantly, though, be a united front.

All decision-makers in the sale need to be on the same page in regard to price and any other conditions. This needs to be agreed upon right from the start and be reaffirmed throughout the marketing campaign, especially before negotiations start, when it matters the most, otherwise you will boycott your sale.

It is best to draw up a written agreement signed by everyone involved before you put any property up for sale.

Negotiating the Agent's Commission

Before signing the listing agreement with an agent, you need to negotiate their commission or selling fee.

Consider the following scenario first:

Your employer is asking you to handle a project with the expectation that you deliver an outstanding result. He then asks you to drop your income by 30%. How would that make you feel?

Would that be an incentive to inspire you to give your absolute best? Probably not. So why would you ask your agent exactly that?

However, you should give it a try and put their negotiation skills to the test.

If an agent is readily willing to drop their income, you need to wonder why, and whether they will be weak in negotiations with your potential buyers to achieve a quick result.

An agent, knowing their craft and self-worth, will be very reluctant to reduce their income and might instead suggest a tiered commission structure if you are willing to price your property within market conditions.

Still, many sellers opt for the cheapest agent and the

lowest marketing plan and assume the best outcome.

You get what you pay for!

Auction Negotiations

During an auction campaign, potential buyers are invited to forward pre-auction offers. However, it needs to be stressed that this is not the time to entertain bargain offers, as only an outstanding tender might entice the seller to accept and call off the auction.

This offer needs to be submitted on a signed Contract of Sale, including a 66W form (cooling-off waiver) and a 10% deposit cheque.

The seller will not make any counter-offers; to them, it is simply a matter of a Yes or No. 'Yes' means the deal is done and 'No' means proceeding towards the auction. It is up to the buyer to increase their offer if they want to buy before auction.

At the auction, the seller avoids underselling with the protection of the reserve price, which is the lowest price the seller is willing to accept. The reserve price is only known to the seller, the agent and the auctioneer. Once the auction has exceeded the reserve price, the highest bid on the fall of the hammer is binding for both buyer and seller.

If the reserve price is not reached, the seller can opt

to accept a lower bid or 'pass the property in', which means the sale will now enter into a Private Treaty negotiation process.

Private Treaty Negotiations

Now it gets tricky.

First of all, your property is expected to be advertised with a price tag, and one motto applies: the first to name a price is the one on the losing end.

Secondly, you will deal with people from all different walks of life, professions, cultural and religious backgrounds and everyone negotiates in their own particular ways.

If you have little or no experience with people from other backgrounds or demographics, there is a high chance that you undersell yourself, or more likely, the deal falls over because of fundamental misunderstandings.

This is the point in time when the skills of an experienced agent come to the rescue.

The reality of Private Treaty sales is that you compete with every single buyer about the price, whilst in an auction sale, you let the buyers compete against each other.

The best offers usually come in at the beginning of a campaign ... often from buyers who have been in the market for a while but haven't found anything suitable yet. Your property might just be the one they have been waiting for; hence they will make their best efforts to outrun any potential competition and present you with a good offer.

Many sellers are tempted to gamble and think that this is an indication of better days still to come. More often, experience shows that the early offers were the best, and serious buyers were turned away when their offer was not accepted.

Always insist in every offer being submitted in writing as verbal offers bear little commitment. Best and final offers should be on a Contract of Sale with a 10% deposit cheque attached.

Furthermore, consider negotiations are not necessarily about the price only, but also about certain purchase conditions, for instance:

- Shorter settlement of a cash buyer
- Extended settlement of a buyer who for some reason needs extra time
- A smaller than a 10% deposit
- Certain inclusions in the sale that are not part of the contract that you are presenting. Keep an open mind and show some flexibility, you are almost at the goal line.

Again, think of Kenny Rogers.

14

The Legal Process

"When everything seems to be going against you, remember that the airplane takes off against the wind, not with it."
Henry Ford

The sale of your property is a legal process.

A solicitor or conveyancer must handle it. They are the only people licensed to give you legal advice.

The latter is a legal profession restricted to property transactions only. They are often faster, as this is all they do and charge less.

However, your sale could be a more complex and complicated matter and might need the resources of a solicitor.

Preparing the Contract of Sale

Your legal representative will discuss with you the terms of the contract, deposit, settlement period, special conditions and inclusions, meaning which fixtures and fittings and other items form part of the sale.

They will also apply for a Title Search, a Section 149 Zoning Certificate and a Water and Sewer Diagram.

Other documents in the contract are the residential or commercial lease (if the property is tenanted), a strata plan (if the property is a townhouse, apartment, office suite etc), strata by-laws and a 66W form (cooling-off Waiver) in case the property is sold under auction terms.

Exchange of Contracts of Sale

There will be two copies of the Contract of Sale: one for you, the seller, and one for the purchaser.

Once the sale has been made, both parties sign their copy of the contract which then will be exchanged. The purchaser pays the relevant deposit: 10% of the purchase price if purchased at auction, 0.25% of the purchase price initially if purchased via Private Treaty, with the balance of the 10% payable at the expiry of the cooling-off period.

If the purchaser decides to rescind the Contract of Sale before the end of the cooling-off period, the 0.25% deposit is forfeited to the seller (NSW – check glossary for other states).

The deposit is paid into your agent's or legal representative's trust account.

Suppose the purchaser wants to rescind an unconditional contract (after the fall of the hammer, after expiry of the cooling-off period or after purchase with a 66W certificate), the 10% deposit will be forfeited to the seller as a compensation for having to repeat the sales process.

Settlement

There is not much for you to do from a legal perspective, apart from informing your bank of the sale, if you have a mortgage, or finishing off certain works that are part of the contract clauses. The rest is all done by your legal representative and by the bank.

Depending on the duration of the settlement period (usually 42 days) you better start packing, as you have to be out of your home on settlement day.

A couple of days before settlement, your agent will take the purchaser through your property for the final settlement inspection.

Make sure you leave the property in a clean condition and without any damages that are not part of the contract or the purchaser can delay settlement, which in turn can affect your next step.

At settlement, the purchaser or their bank will pay the balance of the purchase price. Once the sale has settled, your legal representative will let you know and plan for handing over the money and their invoice.

Now is the time to pop the champagne.

Soon after, your agent will transfer the deposit minus their commission and any other disbursements, as agreed in the listing agreement.

The deal is done.

15

Selling An Investment Property

"Approach each customer with the idea of helping him or her to solve a problem or achieve a goal, not of selling a product or service."
Brian Tracy

Before you decide to sell your investment property, you need to consult your accountant about Capitals Gains Tax (CGT). This is a complex issue which you need to understand to avoid any unexpected tax implications and disappointments after the sale.

If your property is tenanted, have a conversation with your tenant and motivate them to help you with the sale; this might include some rent relief or offer to take care of moving costs if they are willing to leave the premises before the start of the marketing campaign. If they are willing to move on early, you have the chance of giving the property a quick makeover, even if it is just painting, fixing the most obvious flaws, if necessary, and staging.

Tenants have no vested interest in the sale, and many do not make an extra effort to present the property nicely. Presentation is everything, and nothing is worse for your agent to open a property for inspection when it's messy.

Ask the tenant to leave the premises during the inspection times, as their presence might intimidate people inspecting the property. Some tenants also only allow restricted access, which is within their privacy rights.

If a tenant is still well within their lease terms, it might be harder to find a buyer as the tenant comes with the property for the duration of their lease.

Hence, the purchaser needs to be an investor or an owner buyer willing to wait out the existing lease period.

In the Contract of Sale, the box 'Subject to Existing Tenancies' has to be ticked.

If your tenant is on an expired lease, the property can be sold as 'Vacant Possession', as a 30 days 'Notice to Vacate' will be served on the tenant after an unconditional exchange of contracts.

However, in certain economic circumstances a good tenant can be of advantage. It would give potential investors peace of mind not having to worry about finding their first tenant.

Commercial properties are always best sold with a tenant in place, as there are usually long lease terms with optional extension periods. The sales value depends on the percentage Return on Investment.

16

Selling A Deceased Estate

"There is no lotion or potion that will make sales faster and easier for you – unless your potion is hard work."
Jefferey Gitomer

If losing a family member or relative is not traumatic enough, you may now be faced with handling all legal affairs, clearing out their belongings and selling or distributing their assets, including any property.

Unless you want to keep their property or properties for yourself or as an investment, you probably want to sell quickly and for the best possible price, as a vacant property only incurs unnecessary expenses.

Here are some of the essential things you need to

know about winding up an estate in Australia.

How is probate obtained?

If the deceased has left a will, the executor needs to apply to the court for probate, which verifies this will. This can take around four weeks to come through.

Once the grant of probate has been received, the executor then has responsibility for the distribution of the estate to beneficiaries according to the deceased's wishes. The executor is also responsible for hiring deceased estate lawyers and a real estate agent to make sure everything is done legally and transparently.

If the deceased did not leave a will, the process is a little more complicated, as a Letters of Administration document must be obtained from the court.

This has to be done by a family member, and it takes longer than applying for probate.

Consult your Legal Representative

They will tell you the legal steps necessary to prepare the property for sale. Hopefully, there is a will or testament, especially if you are not the only beneficiary.

If there are several beneficiaries, you need to get together, discuss the distribution of the assets and appoint one of you as the executor, unless already stated in the will.

The executor will handle all the following tasks, including the legal process and the sale of assets. For instance, without probate and subsequent title transfer into the executor's name, the property cannot be sold.

This can take several weeks or even months.

Change the locks to all doors immediately as you do not know who else might have access to the property.

Redirect the deceased's mail to the executor's address as you don't want to miss any important letters. It also avoids potential identity theft or the mail ending up all over the front yard.

Gather all important documentation and deal with it as quick as possible, such as:

- Rates notices
- Creditor letters
- Bank account information and mortgage statements
- Home Insurance – contact the provider to inform them of the death and arrange cover

accordingly
- Any other information relating to ownership or property maintenance
- Maintain all payments.

Inform the mortgage holder, local council and water board of ownership changes as you need to stay current with payments until the property is sold.

Even if there is life insurance in place to cover the mortgage upon death, it might take some time for the insurer to release the funds.

While the legal processes are underway, use the time to prepare the property for sale by following Chapter 4 (Preparing Your Property for Sale).

This could take some time, even if the property is in your neighbourhood; things need to be split between the beneficiaries.

Pick an agent by following Chapter 10 (Choosing the Right Agent).

Selling a deceased estate and splitting the proceeds between beneficiaries can be an emotional roller coaster, from fear of missing out to plain greed; again, it might not be easy to keep your emotions in check.

As already mentioned in Chapter 13 (The Art of

Negotiations), everyone concerned with the sale has to be on the same page regarding price and any other conditions.

Agreements need to be made right from the start and be reaffirmed throughout the marketing campaign, especially before negotiations start when it matters the most; otherwise, you will boycott your sale.

It is best to draw up a written agreement signed by everyone involved before you put the property or properties up for sale.

The best selling methods are the Auction sale or Market Buy/Openn Negotiations because of the transparency of the sale for both buyers and beneficiaries.

17

Selling A Property In A Trust

"How you sell matters. What your process is matters. But how your customers feel when they engage with you matters more."
Tiffani Bova

Selling a property in a trust requires guidance from your legal representative.

For a brief overview of what to expect, please read the following article written by *Gerard Basha & Irene Horan:*

"A trustee can be a natural person or a company, but it must have capacity to hold and deal with property.

Companies should check that their constitutional documents allow them this capacity. Before a trustee can exercise a power of sale, it must satisfy itself that it has that power.

Trustees do not have a general power to sell the trust's property because of their paramount obligation to preserve trust property.

The power to sell can arise from the trust instrument, statute (section 38 of the Act) or a Court order.

The trustee must exercise the power according to the standard of care, diligence and skill a prudent person of business would exercise in managing the affairs of another person (section 14A of the Act).

The Sale Process

Before the property can be sold, it may require some work to be done on it.

Trustees have the power to effect repairs and improvement of the property under sections 82 and 82A of the Act.

However, the sale should not be delayed and must take place within a reasonable time for a fair and reasonable price.

The trustee must have the original Certificate of Title

in respect of the property, and the title must be in the trustee's name before the sale to the purchaser can be completed.

If the original Certificate of Title is lost, the trustee must apply for a replacement with Land & Property Information and this may delay completion of the sale.

The trustee will need to engage a real estate agent to market the property and a solicitor to prepare the contract for sale and act on the conveyance.

To ensure the property sells for fair market value and to avoid any breach of trust claim for not obtaining the best price possible, it is prudent to sell by a properly marketed public auction.

If the property is sold by private treaty, the trustee should satisfy itself as to the purchase price by obtaining a valuation from a registered valuer to ensure the property is not sold below market value, which may then invite claims from the beneficiaries."

18

Selling A SMSF (Self-Managed Super Fund) Property

"Most of the important things in the world have been accomplished by people who have kept trying when there seemed to be no hope at all."
Dale Carnegie

If an SMSF is to sell or transfer a property it holds to any party (including a related party such as a member), the applicable legislation requires that this be done on an arm's length basis. The property needs to be valued before the sale, and the purchase price needs to reflect the current market value.

Can I sell property from my SMSF to myself?

Yes, if the transaction is at market value, ie on an arm's-length basis.

Again, you need a documented independent valuation to support the purchase price.

Does my SMSF have to pay Capital Gains Tax?

SMSF capital gains rules state that if you make a net capital gain, it will be included in your SMSF's assessable income.

SMSFs have a flat tax rate of 15%.

Complying SMSFs are entitled to a CGT discount of 1/3 if the relevant asset had been owned for at least a year.

To avoid costly mistakes, talk to your financial planner or accountant about selling your SMSF property before you put it on the market for sale.

19

The Divorce Sale

"Ultimately, we all have to decide for ourselves what constitutes failure, but the world is quite eager to give you a set of criteria if you let it."
J K Rowling

Not all separations end up in 'airing dirty laundry', and the separating partners divide their assets in a fair and amicable way.

Best not mention to the buyer that the reason for the sale is a marriage or relationship break up. It would be more than obvious to any purchaser that the sellers are highly motivated to sell the property as quickly as possible.

In some instances, though, a sometimes lengthy and costly court battle has been proceeding the sale, and both estranged partners want to end the separation process and move on with their lives. They are both mentally and psychologically exhausted from their separation battle.

Here is the tricky part of a divorce sale: emotionally, men often move on more quickly, as for them, the sale is a financial matter.

However, women are more strongly attached to their home, as it means security. When children are involved, women usually feel more uncertain about their future as it will be harder for them to create a new home base. They will have to juggle parenting with work commitments, meaning that earning sufficient income is not easy, especially if they have been a stay-at-home mum during their marriage.

Unfortunately, a failed marriage often follows a communication breakdown and estranged partners cannot work out a reasonable resolution to their problems without the intervention of the legal profession. The longer the legal battle lasts, the more their wealth gets eroded and ends up in the hands of their lawyers.

Therefore, if you are reading this chapter because this is your reality right now, the only advice given is to try to stay reasonable and mediate a solution that avoids costly legal representation.

Regarding the success of your property sale, it is imperative to agree on price and everything else involved in the process before the marketing campaign goes live.

Make it a written agreement and allow your agent to communicate with both of you, as you must be a united front when it comes to decision time.

20

Buying While Selling

"A man is rich in proportion to the things he can afford to let alone."
Henry David Thoreau

Unless you are a cash buyer for your new property, the best advice is to do it one step at a time.

If you have a mortgage right now and you need a loan again, buying before selling can be a risky affair. You do not know what the sales result of your property will be, and you might need bridging finance, which is not cheap.

You will feel pressured to sell quickly, and that might affect the sales price.

Focus on maximising your sales result by following this guide.

Once your property is on the market for sale, you can start house hunting, but wait with any purchase commitments until you know how much money you will have in the bank. Then you can venture out with confidence to secure your next abode.

Ok, you might have to rent somewhere for the short term or negotiate to lease back your property from the purchaser for a certain period. But this is better than losing money on a sale under pressure.

21

Selling With An Unnapproved Structure

"In a crowded marketplace, fitting in is a failure. In a busy marketplace, not standing out is the same as being invisible."

Seth Godin

Unapproved structures usually become a problem for homeowners only when it comes time to sell the property.

These can be pergolas, added rooms or bathrooms, garages, carports, internal changes to the room layout and any renovations that need council approvals etc.

You need to disclose any such uncertified structural

works, not only to your real estate agent, but also to your solicitor/ conveyancer and all potential buyers.

If this is the case with your property you have three options to handle unapproved structures:

1. Attempt to sell the property without council approval with full disclosure
2. Gain retrospective approval
3. Pull down the unapproved structure

Selling without Council Approval

Property with an unapproved structure can be difficult to sell.

First of all you are required to fully disclose all uncertified works in the contract, otherwise the contract can be contested by a potential buyer and you might be up with a fine as well.

A prospective buyer may decide not to proceed with the purchase because they don't want to take on the risk, so the property remains on the market and that means a potential boycott of your sale.

Gain a Retrospective Approval

These are the steps you can take to gain council approval.

1. Ask your local council if you require retro-spective planning and building approval or just building approval. Submit the plans and application/s to council yourself; or
2. Commission a draftsperson to add the structure to your site and floor plan or have new plans drawn up including an elevation drawing.
3. Submit the plans and application/s to council yourself; or
4. Organise for a private building surveyor to undertake a site inspection and assessment to ensure the structure complies with the Building Code of Australia and Australian Standards.
5. Ask the surveyor to submit the application/s to your local council.

Advantages of a Private Site Inspection

The time to gain council approval can be shortened if you use a private building surveyor compared to submitting your plans to council without a surveyor's assessment.

In most cases, a council representative will still want to complete their own site visit but the process is often quicker and less stressful if you know the structure applies before submitting it to council.

Use a building surveyor that does residential

assessments regularly and knows your local council's planning policies and residential design codes.

Retrospective council applications are more common than you may think. Don't panic when you find you need to submit an application.

With the right advice, the process can be made simpler.

Pulling down the Unapproved Structure

Some sellers may decide to pull down a structure that isn't adding significant value to the property.

This might be the easiest way to overcome the problem but depending on the impact it will have on the property it might not be the best solution and you are better off gaining retrospective council approval before putting the property up for sale.

22

Disclosure of 'Material Facts'

""Never let obstacles stop you; figure out a way around it. Be real and authentic. Be passionate aboutwhat you are doing."
Dottie Hermann

All agents have a fiduciary duty to act in the best interest of their clients at all times. Clients can include Vendors, Buyers and Landlords.

Should an agent willingly omit pertinent and relevant information relating to a 'Material Fact', even at the request or instruction of a Vendor or Landlord, they can be exposed to severe penalties that include fines and/or court action and in some cases, loss of licence.

The same law applies if you decide to sell your property yourself.

When buying, prospective purchasers must have all the facts relative to the property they are considering. You and/or your agent must be truthful and must disclose information that is considered a 'Material Fact' in the transaction.

The following kinds of 'Material Facts' are prescribed:

- The property has been subject to flooding from a natural weather event or bush fire within the last 5 years
- The property is subject to significant health and safety risks
- The property is listed on the register of residential premises that contain loose-fill asbestos insulation that is required to be maintained under Division 1A of Part 8 of the *Home Building Act 1989*
- The property was the scene of a crime of murder or manslaughter within the last 5 years
- The property has been used for the purpose of the manufacture, cultivation or supply of any prohibited drug or prohibited plant within the meaning of the *Drug Misuse and Trafficking Act 1085* within the last 2 years
- The property is, or is part of, a building that

contains external combustible cladding:

- To which there is a notice of intention to issue a fire safety order or a fire safety order has been issued requiring rectification of the building regarding the external combustible cladding, or
- To which there is a notice of intention to issue a building product rectification order or a building product rectification order has been issued requiring rectification of the building regarding external combustible cladding

- The property is, or is part of, a building where a development application or complying development certificate application has been lodged under the *Environmental Planning and Assessment Act 979* for rectification of the building regarding external combustible cladding

It is never ok to withhold information just because it is not a 'Prescribed Material Fact'.

If YOU would want to know it, share it.

A not prescribed 'Material Fact' could be a recent normal death or suicide in the house, white ant issues, whether rectified or not, or any other information that could be prescribed as sensitive.

Bring it up in an open discussion with your agent and/ or solicitor before preparing the Contract for Sale and the marketing material.

Don't take this issue lightly, it could cost you the sale of your property and/ or court action and an unnecessary painful fine.

23

Final Word

Dear reader

I hope you enjoyed the chapters of this book and received some helpful tips for successfully selling your home at the best price.

The book is the result of 21 years of selling and purchasing properties, from tiny inner city studio apartments to multi-million dollar houses on large garden blocks.

Some parts of the book are specifically relevant to the Australian property market, especially Chapters 6, 12 and 14 – 18. Hence please enquire about what applies in your state or country in this respect.

However, the basic principles of all the other chapters

should be the same, no matter where you live.

The questions property owners ask in appraisal and listing presentations are often the same, no matter the size and price point of the property.

Like any market, the property market is constantly changing from price volatility to legal frameworks of selling and marketing methods.

It is often hard enough for agents to keep up with the shifts.

On the other hand the basic principles of marketing and selling property and best practice stay the same.

In this context, the book is meant to be an inspiration and you can add your own creativity as you see fit.

But it is best to keep it simple and by following the guidelines outlined in these chapters, you will set yourself up for a successful sale.

Please consider, the longer a property lingers on the market, the less interest of potential buyers it will attract. People will ask themselves why it has not sold yet, whether there is something wrong with the property or whether the price is too high.

The first 3 weeks after your home has come onto the market are the most crucial ones and will yield the most enquiries and attendants at open inspections.

So you need to have 'all of your ducks in a row' to make the most of this initial period.

Whether you want to go it alone or engage an agent is your judgment call.

In this respect, I wish you Happy Selling.

Special Thanks

Before I finish I want to express my heartfelt thanks and gratitude to the people who assisted with writing and completing the book:

Fyonn Wolf for verification of the information and contribution to the content.

Sharon Robins for proof reading and applying some female touch to the script.

Evelyn Kandris for proof reading and improving the readability of the script.

Christine Robinson Global for book formatting, publishing and marketing advice. Christine's expertise and professional assistance were crucial in publishing this book and I could have never done it without her.

About The Author

Introducing Harold Wolf

"A superior communicator and natural 'people person' with a charismatic capacity to build partnerships and long-term relationships whatever the situation, Harold Wolf is an exceptional agent with a proven entrepreneurial flair.

European by birth and Australian by choice, Harold is extremely accomplished at communicating in a clear, concise and friendly manner regardless of background or culture.

With a lifelong love of architecture and property instilled as a small child at his grandfather's knee, Harold's 21 years in real estate have seen him work as a licensed real estate agent, buyer's agent and mortgage broker, giving him a unique skillset and perspective into one of the world's most competitive property markets.

True to his personality, Harold has committed decades to learning everything he can about his chosen industry in order to give his customers the service they deserve.

Progressive and innovative, with an unwavering focus on achieving exceptional results in highly competitive and challenging environments, Harold's impressive track record of success covers a wide variety of fields.

Always up for a challenge and being the best he can be at whatever he turns his mind to, Harold's career experiences are a huge asset for vendors and purchasers alike.

With an outstanding problem-solving ability and self-discipline forged in the military, Harold has been the successful owner of both a building company and an advertising agency, as well as the crewing agent for a major international airline.

As a result, Harold has an incredibly strong work ethic with an intuitive understanding of people and their motivations, especially within a high-pressure environment.

An expert in his field with strong negotiating skills and a deep understanding of processes from advertising design and building to financing and tax requirements, Harold's ability to work with customers to achieve impressive results in competitive markets is without parallel.

Harold is a dynamic individual whose personality energises all those around him.

With a true passion for real estate marketing and sales, combined with a straightforward and honest personality and an astute business acumen, Harold's advice, guidance, insight and approach make him one of Sydney's finest real estate professionals."

~ Andrew Bliss Freelance Writer

Glossary

Agent: A person given permission to act on behalf of a client in the sale, purchase, letting or management of real estate. Agents must be licensed from the relevant state agency.

Amenity: A feature of a neighbourhood, i.e. a public swimming pool, library, school, park etc.

Apartment: A self-contained residential unit that is usually part of a shared building or complex.

Appreciation: The increase in value of real estate caused by external economic factors and market forces.

Appraisal: Written real estate agent's opinion of the market value of a property.

Auction: A public sale in which property is offered for sale through a competitive bidding process.

Body Corporate, also called an **Owner's Corporation:** The main difference between a strata title vs body corporate is that of ownership and legal responsibility.

The owner's corporation or body corporate is responsible to take care of a number of issues related to an internal and external structure of the common area.

Bridging Finance: Finance that is obtained for a short period of time as a 'bridge' to long-term finance. This funding may be required if a home purchase completes before the owner's sale.

Capital Gains Tax (CGT): Most real estate is subject to capital gains tax (CGT). This includes vacant land, business premises, rental properties, holiday houses and hobby farms. Your main residence (your home) is generally exempt from CGT unless you've used it to earn rent or run a business, or it's on more than two hectares of land.

Chattels: Property other than real estate that is included in the sale, including items of furniture.

Commission: A fee or payment made to a real estate agent on completion of the sale of a property.

Contract of Sale: A document that lists the terms and conditions of a property sale between the vendor and the purchaser.

Conveyance: The legal process of transferring the ownership of property from the seller's name to the purchaser's name.

Cooling-Off Period: Allows consumers a time frame during which they can rescind a signed contract with little or no penalty.

New South Wales: 5 business days – Termination penalty 0.25% of purchase price.

Queensland: 5 business days – Termination penalty 0.25% of purchase price.

Victoria: 3 business days – Termination penalty 0.2% of purchase price.

South Australia: 2 business days – Termination penalty up to $100.

Western Australia: No cooling-off period mandatory but can be negotiated between buyer and seller– Termination penalty up to $100.

Tasmania: 3 business days – No termination penalty.

Australian Capital Territory: 5 business days – Termination penalty 0.25% of purchase price.

Northern Territory: 4 business days – No termination penalty.

Deposit: The sum of money normally paid by the buyer at the time of exchange of contracts.

Fittings: Items that can be removed from a property without causing damage or reducing its value, ie paintings, mirrors, curtains, furniture, fridges, washing machines, wall units etc.

Fixtures: Items that are part of the property and which removed, will cause damage to the property and render it incomplete, like bathtubs, toilets, built in wardrobes, hot water heaters, windows, doors etc.

Investment: An asset, like property, that produces income and/ or capital gain.

Listing agreement: A contract between a real estate broker and an owner of real property granting the broker the authority to act as the owner's agent in the sale of the property.

Mortgage: A loan in which property or real estate is used as collateral.

Private Treaty: A private treaty sale is when a property is advertised as being on the market for sale with an asking price and prospective buyers make their offers directly to either the seller or the agent.

Reserve Price: A reserve price is a minimum price a seller is willing to accept from a buyer. In an auction, the seller is not required to disclose the reserve price to potential buyers.

If the reserve price is not met, the seller is not required to sell the item, even to the highest bidder.

Settlement: Legal transfer of ownership of a property from the seller to the buyer.

SMSF: Self-Managed Super Fund.

Advantages

Investment choice
SMSFs offer a wider range of investment options compared to other superannuation funds. With some limited exceptions, a SMSF can invest in virtually anything providing that this also meets the sole purpose test and adheres to the regulations. This includes investing in direct property.

Flexibility & Control
As the members of the fund are also the trustees there is the flexibility to tailor the rules of the SMSF to suit their specific needs and circumstances. This is not available with other superannuation funds.

Effective Tax Management
SMSFs have the same tax rates as other superannuation funds, however through a SMSF you can more easily put in place tax strategies that best benefit you and your situation.

Accountability
Being both the trustee and member means you will be more aware of how your super monies are invested and the performance of those investments.

Costs of Running your Fund
Traditionally, SMSFs were only used by the wealthy due to the high set up and ongoing compliance fees. These days, however, SMSFs are now a much more cost-effective option for all due to advances in technology and competition between service providers.

The cost of running an SMSF can be disadvantageous when the assets held within the SMSF are low in value. As outlined above, many SMSF management costs are fixed and can therefore erode low value SMSFs.

To understand more of the advantages and disadvantages of an SMSF check the following link:

https://www.hrblock.com.au/tax-academy/ smsf-advantages-and-disadvantages

Pooling your Super with Others
SMSFs allow you to pool your superannuation with up to 3 other people. This opens up the opportunity to invest in things an individual may not be able to on their own such as direct property.

Protection from Creditors
Creditors cannot generally access an individual's superannuation. That is unless clawback laws apply where someone has deliberately transferred their assets into a SMSF to escape paying their creditors.

Disadvantages
Although SMSFs carry many benefits they are not suitable for everyone. The disadvantages of having a SMSF include:

Duties & Responsibilities of being a Trustee
When you 'self-manage' your retirement savings you take on the responsibility of all investment decisions; compared to outsourcing this duty to an investment manager within an Industry or Retails Super Fund.

Living Overseas
The majority of a SMSF's members must permanently reside within Australia. If you intend to move overseas permanently or make contributions to your fund while living overseas this could make your fund non-compliant with the law.

Stamp Duty: Stamp duty is a mandatory tax that the state and territory governments levy on a home buyer, whenever they purchase a property.

Strata Title: a form of ownership devised for multi-level apartment blocks and horizontal subdivisions with shared areas.

The word 'strata' refers to apartments being on different levels.

Strata Title Schemes are composed of individual lots and common property.

Valuation: A written report of a property's value – must be provided by a licensed property valuer.

Vendor: Legal property owner.

Zoning Certificate: Also known as a Section 149 or 10.7 planning certificate.

The zoning certificate provides information on any controls, requirements and restrictions that may impact how a property is used, for example, if the property is heritage listed.

Zoning certificates are legal documents issued by the local council.